ANIMALS UNDER THREAT

BENGAL TIGER

IN DANGER OF EXTINCTION!

Richard Spilsbury

Heinemann Library
Chicago, Illinois

© 2004 Heinemann Library
a division of Reed Elsevier Inc.
Chicago, Illinois

Customer Service 888-454-2279

Visit our website at www.heinemannlibrary.com

Design: Jo Hinton-Malivoire and Tokay,
  Bicester, UK (www.tokay.co.uk)
Picture Research: Rosie Garai and Liz Eddison
Originated by Ambassador Litho Ltd.
Printed in China by WKT
Company Limited

08 07 06 05
10 9 8 7 6 5 4 3 2

**Library of Congress Cataloging-in-Publication
Data**
Spilsbury, Richard.
  Bengal tiger / Richard Spilsbury.
    p. cm. -- (Animals under threat)
Summary: Discusses the plight of Bengal tigers
and why they are near extinction, as well as some
of the ways humans can help.
Includes bibliographical references and index.
  ISBN 1-4034-4858-2 (lib. bdg.), 1-4034-5432-9
(Pbk.)
  1. Tigers--Juvenile literature. [1. Tigers. 2.
Endangered species.]
I. Spilsbury, Richard, 1963- II. Title. III. Series.
QL737.C23S586 2004
599.756--dc22

                              2003016135

Acknowledgments

The author and publishers are grateful to the
following for permission to reproduce copyright
material:
pp. 4, 8, 32 J. Van Gruisen/Ardea; p. 5 P.
Perry/FLPA; p. 6 Staffan Widstrand/Bruce
Coleman; pp. 9, 42 Martin Harvey/NHPA; pp. 10,
34 M. Iljima/Ardea; pp. 11, 35 Andy Rouse/NHPA;
pp. 13, 17 Anup Shah/Nature Picture Library;
p. 14 Anup Shah/Getty Images; pp. 16, 41 Digital
Vision; p. 18 T. Whittaker/Corbis; p. 19 M.
Watson/Ardea; p. 20 Arvind Garg/Corbis; p. 21
Ahok Jain/Nature Picture Library; p. 22 S.
Tiwari/Ecoscene; p. 23 Silvestris/FLPA; p. 24
Malcolm Coe/Oxford Scientific Films; p. 25 Bagla
Pallava/Corbis; p. 26 P. Morris/Ardea; p. 27 Adrian
Arbib/Corbis; p. 28 Mike Hill/Oxford Scientific
Films; pp. 29, 38 McDougal/Ardea; p. 30 Tom
Brakefield/Corbis; p. 31 Jagdeep Rajput/Ardea;
p. 33 John Mason/Ardea; p. 36 Paul Lovelace/Rex;
p. 37 Austerman/Oxford Scientific Films; p. 39
Richard Spilsbury; p. 43 Tudor Photography.

Cover photograph reproduced with permission of
Mike Powles/Oxford Scientific Films.

Special thanks to Fiona Sunquist for her review of
this book. Ms. Sunquist is co-author, along with
Dr. Mel Sunquist, of *Tiger Moon: Tracking the Great
Cats in Nepal* and *Wild Cats of the World.*

Disclaimer

Some words are shown in bold, **like
this.** You can find out what they mean
by looking in the glossary.

Contents

The Bengal Tiger

The tiger is the biggest and probably most recognized cat in the world. Of all the big cats—such as lions, leopards, and jaguars—only tigers have striped coats. Tigers are part of a large group, or **genus,** called *Panthera*, which also includes big cats such as the leopard. All tigers belong to one smaller group or **species** called *tigris*. Within this group there are five surviving **subspecies.** Each one gets its name from the different part of Asia where it lives or was first named. The five subspecies are called Bengal, Sumatran, Siberian, South China, and Indo-Chinese tigers.

Tigers of each subspecies look slightly different. Siberian tigers are generally the biggest, sometimes over 10 feet (3 meters) long, with fewer stripes than the others. Each individual tiger of any subspecies, however, has a unique stripe pattern, like a person's fingerprints. This means each tiger can be distinguished from any other tiger.

Tiger ancestors

To find the **ancestors** of modern tigers, you must look back 60 million years to the age of the dinosaurs. The small weasel-like **mammals** that lived on Earth at this time were totally different than tigers. Over millions of years, their **descendants** gradually became the distinctive bear, dog, and cat families recognized today. Fossil evidence suggests that the earliest tigers appeared two million years ago. Since then, tigers have spread over nearly all of Asia.

Bengal tigers usually have a bright reddish-orange coat, with a creamy white belly. Their thin stripes are mostly vertical and are black, gray, or brown.

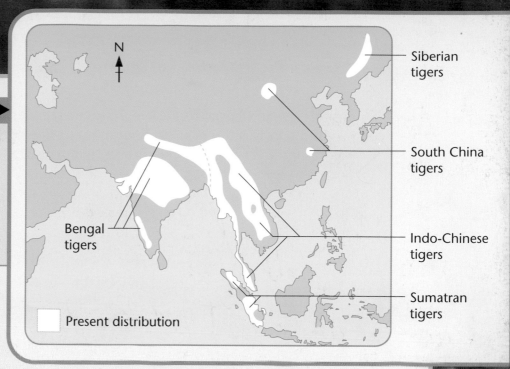

The five subspecies of tiger live in different parts of Asia. The Bengal tiger is the most common.

N

Siberian tigers

South China tigers

Indo-Chinese tigers

Sumatran tigers

Bengal tigers

Present distribution

Changing fortunes

Tens of thousands of years ago, the tiger species was one of the most dominant of the major **predators** of Asia. Like all animals, they lived more successfully in some areas than others, because of things such as changes in climate and availability of **prey.** Over time, tigers became different enough from each other in different locations that eight separate subspecies were identified.

Populations of all eight tiger subspecies remained stable for a long time. But then humans started to kill them in large numbers by hunting and by changing the places where they lived. In the last 100 years, three subspecies—the Caspian, Bali, and Java tigers—have become **extinct** because of human activities. The remaining five subspecies of tiger are **endangered.** This means that unless special care is taken to look after them, they could also become extinct. The rarest, the South China tiger, has a wild population of only around 20 to 30 tigers and is very close to extinction.

Bengal tigers

This book focuses on Bengal tigers. They were first named in the state of Bengal in western India. There are more wild Bengal tigers than tigers of all the other subspecies put together. But their population is falling each year. Many people are already trying to protect them. By examining the lives and habits of these big cats and the threats they face, this book also shows what people can do to save the tigers.

Tiger Country

Nearly all wild Bengal tigers live in India. The Bengal tiger is often called the Indian tiger. Some Bengal tigers live outside India in neighboring countries. There are small populations in southern Nepal, western Myanmar, Bhutan, and Bangladesh.

Tiger habitat

Bengal tigers live in a range of different **habitats** in these countries, but all the habitats have certain features in common. A proper tiger habitat must provide some type of dense plant cover. Something to hide behind is vital for this **predator.** It must be able to **stalk** its **prey** without being seen. Tiger habitats must also provide the large amounts of food and water the tigers need to survive.

Tigers in India

There are populations of Bengal tigers in 18 of the 26 states, or regions, of India. About a third of all Bengal tigers live in the central Indian state of Madhya Pradesh.

Madhya Pradesh contains around one-fifth of India's forest area and large populations of wild guar (a kind of cattle), a favorite tiger prey.

For a tiger to survive, it must live in the same habitats as the animals that it feeds upon.

Bengal tigers can live in different kinds of forests. Some live in humid, **tropical** forests with thick, lush undergrowth, often called jungle. Others live among tall grasses such as bamboo or in open **deciduous** forests. These types of habitat change more with the seasons, especially in the annual rainy season called the **monsoon.**

Bengal tigers have adapted to life in different types of climate. Some live in Himalayan valleys 9,800 feet (3,000 meters) above sea level that are covered in thick snow each year. Others live in hot, mosquito-infested swamps, or in dry **scrub** areas on the edge of deserts.

Sundarbans tigers

The Sundarbans is a swampy area where the land meets the sea, near the mouth of the Ganges River in eastern India. The habitat is one of wooded islands and areas of mangrove swamps. Mangroves are plants that thrive in seawater. Their tangled roots stick out of the thick, salty mud. Many young fish and crabs live in the warm shallow water among the mangroves. These are prey for many birds and crocodiles. Several hundred tigers also live in this unusual habitat. They are strong swimmers, so they can travel among the many small islands in search of prey and shelter.

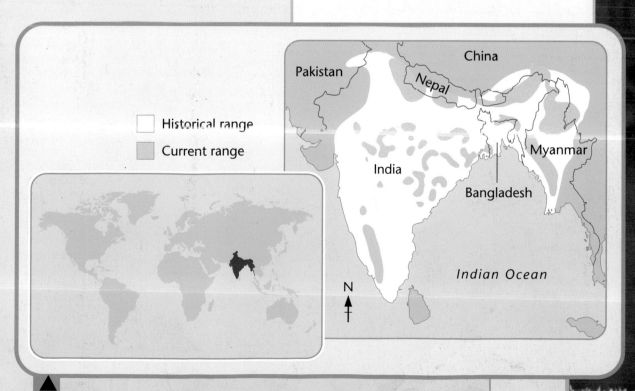

Bengal tigers now live only in small groups throughout India and neighboring countries.

Tiger Populations

There is much debate about how many Bengal tigers there are in the wild. Most scientists estimate that there are between 3,200 and 4,500. Over 2,500 of these are in India. With so few tigers, you might think that they could be counted quite accurately. The problem is that although they are big **mammals,** tigers are very secretive. They move around mostly at night, often in dense forests, and they are good at hiding. So how do scientists estimate how many tigers there are?

Signs of tigers

One way to find out if tigers are in the area is to look for signs they have left. These might be leftover parts of **carcasses** from their kills, piles of dung, or pugmarks (footprints). But the presence of these signs does not help us to know how many tigers made them. One thing scientists do know is that there is a limit to how many kills one tiger makes in a short period of time. So, a lot of carcasses spread over a wide area may mean that many tigers are around in that specific area. But how many tigers are there?

Pugmarks

Scientists have estimated, or guessed, the numbers of tigers by using pugmarks (pawprints) to recognize individuals. Tigers have big fleshy pads on their paws, which cushion their feet and help them to walk quietly when hunting. A male has

The stripes on a tiger help to keep its large body hidden in the vertical shade patches between tall plants.

larger paws than a female. So, it is possible to know if a specific pugmark was made by a male or a female. But beyond that, pugmarks do not provide accurate information.

Problems With Pugmarks

Some scientists and tiger reserve staff still use pugmarks to count tigers, but there are problems with this method. Pugmarks can only be seen clearly on certain types of ground. They are visible in damp mud but not in dry grass or fallen leaves. So they cannot be used to recognize tigers in certain **habitats.**

In the Sundarbans, the tidal flow from the ocean washes over a lot of pugmarks and changes them or covers them completely. During a tiger count in 1997, pugmarks from nine tigers were reported in one area, but local people reported seeing many more tigers.

Traps and bait

There are two better ways of counting tigers. Camera traps are hidden cameras with flashes that take pictures when an animal moves

▲ The plaster cast of an old pugmark is compared with new pugmarks to check which tiger has passed through.

through a light trigger. The stripe pattern on each tiger is used to identify it. The equipment for this method can be expensive and not all tiger conservation groups have the money for this. The second way is to leave fresh carcasses of goats or cattle as bait to attract tigers. Observers can then identify individual tigers from a hidden position nearby.

The Body of a Tiger

Bengal tigers have special features that help them survive in their **habitat.** Adults can be nearly 10 feet (3 meters) long and weigh over 440 pounds (200 kilograms). But like most cats, they are very muscular and agile, with good balance. They can leap up to 33 feet (10 meters), swim several miles, and sometimes climb trees. A tiger's legs are thick and strong. Their paws are up to 12 inches (30 centimeters) across. Each paw has four large toes. The front paws have a fifth, smaller toe higher up the leg. A sharp, curved claw sticks out of each toe when the tiger stretches its paws. Claws are used to hold on to its **prey** and to scratch. The claws tuck back in when not in use to stop them from being worn or damaged.

Tigers pull back their cheeks and lips to expose their large canine teeth.

A tiger's mouth

Tigers are **carnivores,** with short and powerful jaws. They have 30 large teeth. The four long, pointed canine teeth are used to stab and grip prey, and are up to 4 inches (9 centimeters) long. Wider carnassial teeth at the back of the jaw have sharp ridges that help cut through flesh and bone.

A tiger's tongue is long and coated with tiny, sharp bumps. These bumps make it rough enough to lick hair or even skin off prey if a lot of force is applied. A tiger also uses its tongue more gently to groom (lick and clean) its own hair, and to lap up water to drink.

Tiger senses

Just like people, tigers use their senses to understand and react to the world around them. Two of their senses, sight and hearing, are especially well developed.

Tigers' eyes point forward, like those of many **predators.** This allows them to see what is moving in front of them and judge how far away it is. This is called binocular vision. Many prey animals have eyes on the sides of their heads so they can see all around them to spot approaching predators.

At night, when tigers usually hunt, their vision is about six times better than a human's. This is because they have a reflective coating inside their eyes that reflects the small amount of light onto their sensitive **retinas.**

Tigers, like other cats, have sharp hearing that can pick up soft sounds. They can tell if leaves in the undergrowth are rustling because of a breeze or if an animal is brushing against them. They can twist their ears in the direction of sounds to quickly locate possible prey.

A cat's whiskers

Whiskers are thick, sensitive hairs that grow mostly on a cat's upper lip, but also above its eyes and on other parts of its body. Cats use their whiskers mostly at night to help feel where objects are, including prey. They can also use them to judge the width of spaces they are moving through.

▲ If the whiskers above its eyes are touched by struggling prey, a tiger closes its eyes for protection. Whiskers around its mouth give advance hints of where to bite.

A Supreme Hunter

Types of prey

Bengal tigers usually hunt wild deer, called chital or sambar, and wild pigs, which are often much smaller than the tigers. They can also hunt much larger **mammals**, such as water buffalo and gaur, which is up to 6.5 feet (2 meters) tall. Tigers are not very picky eaters. They sometimes catch crocodiles, bears, leopards, porcupines, fish, birds, or even locusts.

Adult Bengal tigers are not hunted by any other animals. They are called apex **predators.** That means they are at the top of the **food web** in their **habitat.** Tigers hunt a wide range of **prey** in order to get enough to eat. They hunt mostly at night, in the early morning, or late evening.

Tigers take easy options if they can, usually hunting slower-moving, weaker prey. It takes a lot of energy to hunt. Tigers do what they can to make sure that a hunt will be successful.

How tigers hunt

Tigers hunt on their own. They look for prey from the cover of bushes, trees, and long grass. When they spot prey, they carefully **stalk** it. When stalking, a tiger keeps its head steady, its eyes focused on its prey, and its body low. It stays downwind (positioned so that the wind blows from the prey toward the tiger). A whiff of tiger scent would alert the prey to its presence.

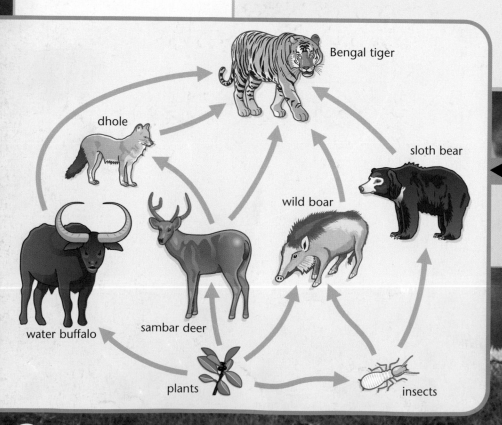

Bengal tiger

dhole

sloth bear

wild boar

water buffalo

sambar deer

plants

insects

Bengal tigers are at the top of the food web.

The rush

When the tiger is close enough to its prey it suddenly rushes at the animal. It uses its long, heavy tail to keep its balance as the prey changes direction. If the tiger attacks from too far away, the prey will probably escape. Tigers can run fast only over short distances of up to about 82 feet (25 meters).

Tigers are excellent hunters, but only one out of ten tiger rushes is successful. When the rush is timed right, the tiger uses its strong front legs and sharp claws to grab the back of the neck, shoulders, or chest of its prey. If the prey is big, the tiger may grab its ankles to trip it. Once the prey has been brought down, the tiger bites it in the throat, which **suffocates** the prey. Smaller prey is killed with a bite to the back of the neck. Tigers can be injured by bites, kicks, and scratches as they do this.

The carcass

Tigers kill large prey about once a week. They carry or drag the prey's **carcass** to shelter or near water. They can drag a carcass over distances of up to 550 yards (500 meters). Tigers eat all parts of the carcass. They can eat up to 88 pounds (40 kilograms) of meat at one meal. After eating, they often have a drink of water. If any of the carcass is left over, they hide it under grass or leaves and come back to it later.

Nearly all cats are solitary animals. They spend most of their time alone. Each adult tiger lives in a particular area of its **habitat** all year. This area provides it with enough food, shelter, and water holes. It is called a **home range.**

Bengal tigers, like other big cats, live in large home ranges of between 4 and 97 square miles (10 and 250 square kilometers). A home range is usually smaller in places where there is plenty of **prey,** but larger where there are fewer prey animals. Home ranges can also change in size during the year. For example, Bengal tigers that live by the Himalayas move through a bigger area during the snowy winter than they do in summer to find enough prey.

Keeping other tigers out

A tiger will generally try to keep other tigers completely out of its home range or a part of it. An area that an animal keeps other animals out of is called a **territory.** A tiger makes a territory so it has exclusive rights to the prey and to any **breeding** opportunities. Males make territories because they contain females they want to mate with. There may be several female home ranges within one male's territory. Females have territories to keep other tigers away from their cubs because they may harm them.

A water hole is an important part of a Bengal tiger's home range. It uses the water to drink and to cool down. The water may also attract prey.

Working out ranges

Scientists work out tiger ranges by drugging individual tigers so they go to sleep and then fitting them with radio collars. After the animal wakes up, its movements can be followed using radio receivers. Then, its location can be marked on a map. Over time, a pattern of regular movement becomes clear and range boundaries can be identified.

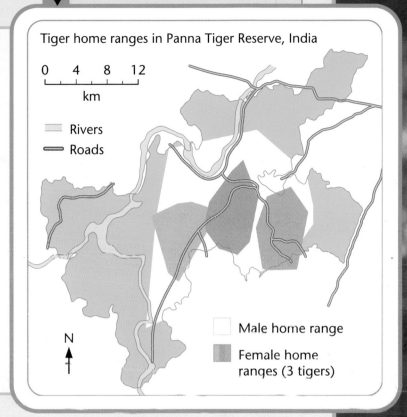

In Panna Tiger Reserve, three females live within the home range of one male.

Tiger home ranges in Panna Tiger Reserve, India

0   4   8   12
km

Rivers
Roads

N

Male home range

Female home ranges (3 tigers)

Marking territories

Tigers, like most other cats, **mark** their territories to show others where the boundaries are. They mostly mark with scent. They spray urine on tree trunks or rocks and leave piles of dung, called scats. Sometimes they mark using visual signs. They scratch tree trunks with their claws or scrape together piles of loose leaves and soil. To make sure other tigers do not miss these signs, they often use visual and scent signals together. When tigers scratch a tree, they also rub it with a scent made in the **glands** between their toes.

Once boundaries are marked, tigers patrol them by walking along the scent trails. They may replace any smells that are fading.

No range

Tigers establish their home ranges on a first-come-first-served basis. Some tigers, especially young adult males, will not have a home range until an existing range owner dies. They live in small zones between ranges and keep out of the way of other tigers. However, young adult females sometimes share a home range with their mother.

Courtship and Communication

Roaring

Like other big cats, a tiger uses muscles and elastic ligaments to stretch its throat wide open to make loud roars. It twists its ears back and narrows its eyes as it roars.

A tiger's roar can be heard up to 2 miles (3 kilometers) away.

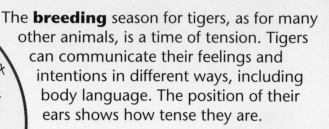

The **breeding** season for tigers, as for many other animals, is a time of tension. Tigers can communicate their feelings and intentions in different ways, including body language. The position of their ears shows how tense they are.

Young adult males will only breed if they have their own **territory.** Therefore, they are more likely to risk entering another male's territory during the breeding season.

The breeding cycle begins with courtship, when animals select and attract a mate. Tigresses (female tigers) first go into estrus. This means they are ready to mate and become pregnant. They communicate their condition by roaring and moaning repeatedly. They also **mark** their territory with a mixture of urine and fluid from special **glands.**

The male tiger regularly smells scent marks left by other tigers. However, the scent left by a female in estrus is different. The male responds in a special way called the flehmen or grimace response.

During flehmen, the male tiger's nose wrinkles; his eyes close; his chin is raised; his mouth opens; and his tongue lolls out. He is testing the scent using a sensitive pit in the roof of his mouth called the Jacobson's organ.

Rival males

The estrus signals made by a female may attract more than one male. If two males meet, the trespasser usually backs away. Sometimes both stay and test each other's nerve with a series of displays. Each display has a particular meaning. They challenge each other first by staring, then by showing their teeth and flaring their whiskers. If neither backs down, they hiss and grow louder and louder.

Tigers usually rely on display to settle arguments. Fighting with their sharp claws, teeth, and immense strength could easily result in serious injury or death.

Meeting a mate

When a male and a female meet up to mate, they are very careful at first. These solitary animals are not often in the company of strangers. They snarl and snap at each other for a while, gradually moving closer. Eventually the female trusts the male enough to start to nuzzle, lick, and rub him. She is now ready to mate.

Seasonal breeding

Bengal tigers enjoy a season of plenty during the Indian fall. The spring to summer **monsoon** rains have watered the dry land, encouraging many plants to grow. Like most animals, **herbivores,** such as deer, use the period of plentiful food to breed. As a result, there is a lot of prey for tigers in fall and winter, and they too can breed. They usually mate between November and April. They give birth three to four months later.

▲ *Bengal tigers rear up on their back legs to fight using their claws and teeth.*

Young Tigers

Pregnant tigresses usually give birth to two or three cubs. A mother chooses a lair—a safe, sheltered spot to give birth. It may be in a cave, a rocky crevice, or just space within dense plant cover. The newborn cubs are covered in short, striped hair and weigh around 2 pounds (1 kilogram) each. Their eyes are closed and do not open until they are around two weeks old. The first danger they face is starvation. Although their mother cares for them by licking their coats clean, she does not help them **suckle.** It can take a cub up to four hours to find a nipple.

A tigress's milk is a complete food for her cubs for the first eight weeks of life. It helps the cubs grow and develop quickly. The milk even provides the water they need.

Growing up

Cubs start to come out of the lair when their eyes open. They are curious but also cautious and stay close to their mother. If she leaves them to hunt, she makes sure they are somewhere safe, such as the old lair or a new shelter. Because they cannot walk very fast, she often carries the cubs by gripping the loose skin on their necks and head in her teeth.

The cubs start to eat meat brought by their mother when they are around two months old. They suckle less and less. They stop suckling completely around four months later.

Independence

The cubs learn to hunt food for themselves in stages. At first their mother brings them to a **carcass.** She may help by ripping open tough skin to reveal the softer meat inside. Later, she partly kills an animal and they learn how to kill with a **suffocating** hold. Finally, the cubs start to hunt small **prey.** They improve their technique mostly by watching their mother but sometimes also their father. Cubs become independent of their mother at between eighteen months and two years, when they usually find their own **home ranges.**

Natural dangers

Tiger cubs face many natural dangers, from **predators** to fires and floods. About half of all cubs do not survive more than two years. A cub away from the safety of its mother, or out of hiding, may become prey for a hyena, a leopard, or a wild dog. Cubs are sometimes killed by adult male tigers trying to take over **territory** belonging to the cubs' father. As the cubs grow, some of these dangers lessen. Tigers may live for as long as 20 years.

Runt of the litter

One cub, called the runt, is usually smaller than the others. Some runts die at birth, but many others die later from starvation or from being easier prey for predators.

Play is a vital way for tiger cubs to learn how to survive as adults. Rough play like this helps them develop useful hunting skills.

Conflict Between Tigers and People

Adult Bengal tigers face no wild **predators** unless they are weakened by injury, illness, or old age. However, there is one **species** that is so dangerous that all tigers, whatever their age and strength, are at risk: human beings.

A human might not appear to be much of a threat to a tiger. An adult tiger is bigger and stronger. It has far more lethal natural weapons—teeth and claws. However, people have developed weapons that can kill any tiger, and machines that can completely change a tiger's **habitat.** These dangers from people are not faced by Bengal tigers alone. Many other wild animals are also at risk. There is usually one major reason why animals become **endangered.** People want to take over or use the wild places where they live.

Population explosion

There are more than six billion people on Earth. The population is expanding rapidly and is predicted to reach seven billion by 2015. There are many reasons for this. One is improvements in health care. As a result, more diseases can be cured and illnesses treated. So, more babies survive, and older people live longer. As the population increases, people need more space to live, work, and to get food and water. This means they put more pressure on the environment.

When people cut down forests to plant crops or graze animals, there is less space for tigers and their prey.

Fishers in the Sundarbans often wear human face masks in the hope of scaring off a man-eating tiger approaching from behind.

Conflict

As areas of the Bengal tiger's habitat get smaller, the tigers find it more and more difficult to find enough food. As people and tigers live closer together, conflicts and problems arise. **Livestock,** such as cattle, buffalo, or goats are easy **prey** for hungry tigers.

A tiger's hunting skills help it get past most human guards. Some tigers even get used to eating mostly livestock. It takes less effort to catch a cow than to **stalk** and rush wild pigs and other quick prey. People try to scare off tigers by moving in large groups through the forest carrying lit torches or banging drums. If this does not scare off the tigers, people sometimes kill them.

Man-eaters

Some tigers get so desperate for a meal that they prey on people. Man-eaters are usually tigers that are too old or injured to hunt, but they can also be fitter, younger animals. Catching unarmed people is easier than hunting stronger, faster wild animals. Man-eating tigers are rare, but they often kill more than once. There are several known man-eaters in the Sundarbans National Park in India that have often killed fishers and people collecting wild honey.

Poaching

Poaching means illegally killing or taking wild animals. One example is fishing salmon from a stretch of river that belongs to someone else. Another is killing **endangered** Bengal tigers in protected **reserves.**

It is difficult to know how many tigers are poached because no one knows exactly what the population is, and poachers are secretive. However, it is estimated that one Bengal tiger is killed every day.

Why people poach

People poach Bengal tigers because illegal traders have offered them money for tiger skins, bones, and other body parts. The traders approach people who are poor and who live in or near areas where tigers live, because they know a lot about the **habitat.** The poachers need the money, so they are prepared to risk the punishment of being fined and jailed.

How people poach

Poachers use different ways to kill tigers. The most common way is to put poison in fresh **carcasses** of **livestock** such as cows or water buffalo. In dry seasons the poachers poison the water in small forest pools where tigers drink.

Poaching is one of the main reasons why Bengal tigers are endangered.

The risk and the reward

- A poacher is paid around $50 for killing a tiger. A trader can sell the tiger parts for $3,000 to $6,000.
- If someone is caught poaching a tiger, the penalty for breaking the law is a fine of about $160 and a minimum of one year in jail. Because of difficulties enforcing laws, only one or two people have ever been convicted of killing a tiger in India.

Special steel traps are also used. They are set along trails where tigers might walk and are covered so they cannot be seen. If a tiger steps in a trap, it closes on the tiger's leg. Usually the tiger is hurt so badly that it dies.

In some areas, poachers use hidden electrical wires to electrocute tigers. They also use guns in remote parts of reserves where the gunshots cannot be heard by **wardens.**

Smuggling routes

The valuable parts of the tiger are **smuggled** to where they can be sold. Tiger bones are often hidden among those from legally killed animals, such as cattle. The bones are used to make glue and fertilizers (which are nutrients used to make plants grow better).

Traders smuggle Bengal tiger parts from India into China across the mountains. They trade them with nomads (people who move from place to place), who in turn sell them to other people in China who make traditional medicines.

Tiger parts are highly valued in traditional medicines. Bones are ground into powder and made into pills and potions to treat diseases such as rheumatism. Eyeballs are used to treat epilepsy, and whiskers are used to treat toothaches. Tiger medicines are sold illegally in shops and clinics around the world.

▲ *Tiger traps can be so strong that they take six adult men to open them.*

Dealing with Poaching

In many places in India, tigers are protected in **reserves. Wardens** and guards patrol the reserves to keep **poachers** away. However, the poachers are often better equipped than the guards and can be very dangerous. They have guns and explosives and fast vehicles to get away quickly. They often use cell phones to warn each other of possible detection.

Often, there are only a few wardens for each reserve. This makes it difficult to find the poachers. This problem is sometimes made worse when local people help poachers. They may help **track** tigers or protect the poachers. This may be because they are frightened of them, or have been paid to help, or because their **livestock** will be safer with fewer tigers around.

Stopping poachers

Poaching can be stopped, but it takes money to supply and employ reserve workers. Reserve workers should be encouraged to arrest poachers and seize dead tiger parts so they cannot be sold. Any dead tigers found should be examined carefully to see if they were poisoned or died naturally. The best long-term solution is to encourage both poachers and local people to change their attitudes and look after the tigers.

Reserves are only effective protection for tigers if there are enough wardens with good equipment.

Stopping the bone traders

The trade in Bengal tiger bones had become a major problem in India by the 1980s. Populations of other tiger **subspecies** in countries such as China were decreasing. Demand was growing for traditional medicines made with tiger parts, so poaching increased elsewhere. Some traders in tiger parts are rich businesspeople who have connections with important people in different countries. This often allows them to avoid capture and punishment.

The bones, skins, and claws of around 250 tigers have been seized in India since 1993.

The best way to stop international traders is to use the law. Undercover investigators make contact with traders and track their **smuggling** routes. They inform police and **customs** officers, who seize and destroy tiger parts and punish the traders. However, international laws have to be agreed to and enforced worldwide. This will help make sure that international traders are punished more strictly and stop trading. It helps when investigators use the latest ways of distinguishing between tiger and cattle bones, such as DNA **(gene)** testing.

Changing demand

Tiger medicines are in demand partly because they are an alternative to Western medicines, but also because they are a traditional custom. People all over the world, including doctors and scientists, say that tiger parts are no more effective as cures than, for example, buffalo parts. They say that it is time to change a tradition that is threatening tigers with **extinction**.

Tiger Hunting in the Past

In the past people hunted tigers for different reasons. Some people were paid to kill tigers to protect other people. In India in the 18th and 19th centuries, there were professional tiger hunters called *shikaris*. They made their living by accompanying travelers through tiger **habitats** and by helping villagers get rid of tigers. They often wore a tiger skin, which they claimed gave them magical powers. They carried a shield, a spear, or a sword. *Shikaris* built platforms in trees called *machans,* where they would wait to spear tigers. They also dug and covered pit traps containing spears for unsuspecting tigers to fall into.

Sport of kings

Tiger hunting was also a royal sport. To Indian kings, killing a tiger was a proof of their power. Ancient custom said that a ruler should kill 109 tigers! Kings never hunted alone. Hundreds or even thousands of helpers made sure the hunt would be successful.

The king often rode on the back of an elephant, in an ornate saddle platform called a *howdah.* Some helpers rode on other elephants, loading rifles for the king. Others, called beaters, walked in groups through the forest or grass shouting, letting off fireworks, or beating drums. Their noise flushed out any wild animals, including tigers, from the dense vegetation toward the king and others with guns.

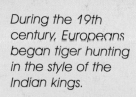
During the 19th century, Europeans began tiger hunting in the style of the Indian kings.

British in India

To the British people who came to India as **colonizers** in the early 19th century, hunting tigers was partly seen as a public service. They had better guns than the local people, so they were more likely to be successful. Local people looked to British soldiers or police officers to act as *shikaris*. Some skilled *shikaris* became legendary, because they removed well-known man-eaters.

In the late 1800s and early 1900s, tiger hunting became a popular sport among rich British people in India. Hunts were also big social events, like parties. People competed over who could shoot the most tigers.

It was not unusual for people to kill more than 100 tigers each. To show how brave they were, they proudly displayed their trophies, such as tiger skins with stuffed heads displaying snarling teeth, which they used as rugs. The demand for these items and for fashions using tiger skins spread to Europe and other parts of the world, and the tiger population decreased rapidly.

Shooting film not bullets

Jim Corbett grew up in India, learned to shoot well, and killed his first tiger at the age of eight. He later became famous as a shikari. **He tracked** and killed the Champawat Tiger, a man-eater that had killed over 400 people. Corbett killed many tigers, but he also learned about them and increasingly took photos rather than shots. In 1936, distressed at how rare the tigers were becoming, he set up the Corbett National Park in India to help conserve tigers.

Destroying Tiger Habitats

One of the greatest threats to Bengal tigers, after **poaching,** is the destruction of their **habitat.** In the past, Asia was covered with large areas of forest. Today most of this forest has disappeared because of the growing human population. Between 1973 and 2003, the number of people in India rose by nearly 500 million and the number of **livestock** increased by 100 million.

Many trees and other plants are cut down for lumber to build houses, for firewood fuel, and for livestock food. Other areas are cleared to provide land for farming and housing. Farms and houses need water and power. This means more land is cleared to build dams and canals for **irrigation,** power plants for electricity, and roads to travel on. Habitat is also destroyed to dig mines and build factories. Some of these industries add to the problems for wild animals by **polluting** rivers, lakes, and the air.

For some people, forests are a supply of wood they can cut down and sell, not special habitats occupied by different plants and animals.

The price of development

Many people see habitat destruction as an acceptable result of **development,** which improves the lives of others. For example, building a factory on newly cleared land may bring jobs to the local people. So, a lot of habitat destruction is officially approved. In 2000 the Indian government approved a project with funding from the World Bank to build the Kotku Dam, which will provide water, power, and jobs for local people. However, it will also drown the best forests in a tiger reserve called Palamau.

Bengal tigers are running out of habitat in India.

The importance of tiger habitat

Tiger habitats are important to the environment for several reasons. One of the most critical reasons is water. Forests and jungles in India are prime **water catchment areas.** When rain falls onto forests and their surrounding hills, it soaks into the topsoil—the ground's fertile surface.

Some water filters into rivers, water holes, and dams, but some filters into the ground. This groundwater provides water for wells used by many Indian people. Without trees, topsoil washes away and rainwater runs off the hills. This often causes flooding, and groundwater supplies are not replaced.

Tiger habitat is also important for many other animals and plants that in turn benefit humans. For example, local people harvest seasonal foods, such as honey and fruit, and plants that can be used as medicines.

Links in a food chain

A Bengal tiger's survival is linked with the lives of other organisms in its habitat. Tigers will only have enough **prey** to hunt if the prey can find enough to eat. Deer, for example, need grass, tender shoots, and wild fruit to eat. Tigers and other **predators** are useful to prey groups. When they hunt weaker, diseased, or older members of a herd of prey, the fitter, stronger survivors breed and improve the overall health of the herd.

Fragmented Tiger Populations

Today, the remaining wild Bengal tigers live in many different places. But the patches of tiger **habitat** are surrounded by land that the tigers cannot live on. This may be because the land has been **developed** with roads and towns, or because people have hunted most of the wild pigs and deer, so there is not enough **prey** for tigers.

Fragments

In the past, areas where tigers lived covered large areas. Along the border between India and Nepal, for example, there were once thousands of miles of continuous forests where tigers lived. Today, there are four separate tiger populations, each with between 15 and 45 tigers. They are cut off from one another by farms and villages. The tigers in these fragmented populations cannot mix. It is as if they are trapped on islands surrounded by ocean and are unable to swim.

Small, isolated populations of Bengal tigers are at risk of becoming lost for ever. Many kinds of chance events, such as a drought or a flood, could wipe them out.

Population fact

Scientists estimate that there need to be at least 300 tigers in a population to stop inbreeding. Most populations of Bengal tigers contain fewer than 100 individuals.

*When animals such as tigers are split up into small groups, they are in greater danger of **extinction**. People can help by creating corridors, or narrow strips, of suitable habitat between the populations of tigers. Tigers can then travel from one area to another to **breed**.*

Too small

There can be problems within small populations of tigers. If there are only a few males and one dies, there may not be enough other males around to mate with the females. This means they will not have cubs. If there are many males in the population, they are more likely to fight and be injured as they attempt to control more of the available space.

When tigers in an isolated population **inbreed** over several generations, the tiger population becomes weaker, or less able to survive changes. This is because the tigers begin to have very similar **genes.** For example, if a disease spreads through the group and all the tigers share a low resistance to it, they might all die. If there is more variety in the genes within the group, some tigers will be affected less than others. These tigers will survive, and pass on their resistance to their young.

Inbred tigers become weaker in different ways. Some are infertile (unable to breed) and others have physical problems, such as crossed eyes or a cleft palate (a split in the roof of the mouth), that affect their ability to hunt.

Saving Tiger Habitats

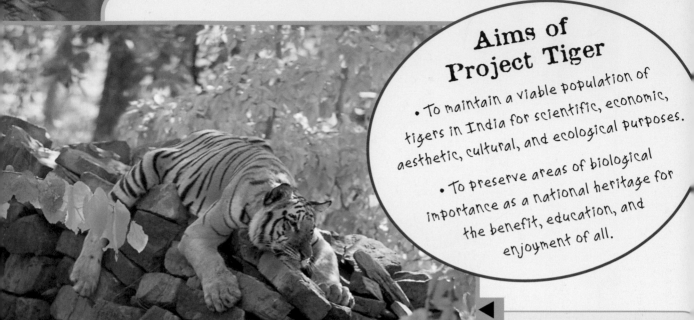

Aims of Project Tiger

- To maintain a viable population of tigers in India for scientific, economic, aesthetic, cultural, and ecological purposes.

- To preserve areas of biological importance as a national heritage for the benefit, education, and enjoyment of all.

Bengal tigers are protected among the ruined palace walls in Ranthambhore Tiger Reserve, India.

In India there is a long tradition of preserving areas of Bengal tiger **habitat.** In the past this was to keep the areas well stocked with wild animals, such as tigers, just for kings and other important people to hunt. Today these areas are preserved to save the wild animals by keeping out the **poachers** and land **developers.**

Project Tiger

A tiger population survey in 1972 confirmed the worst fears of international conservation workers. There were fewer than 2,000 Bengal tigers left in India. In 1973 Project Tiger was launched by the Indian government, with the support of international conservation organizations such as the World Wildlife Fund (WWF) and The World Conservation Union (IUCN). The tiger became India's new national symbol. Nine tiger **reserves** were set up, and more followed in later years. Each reserve is patrolled by **wardens** to stop poaching. The hope was that tiger populations in these areas would increase and that eventually tigers would spread out into the surrounding areas.

Changing emphasis

When Project Tiger reserves were set up, local people living in these areas were badly affected. Often they had to move their homes to new places. They were not allowed to work in or collect wild food from the forests, as they traditionally had, because the land was given over to tigers. This created frustration and resentment about the reserves. Over time, people have increasingly moved back into these reserves, squeezing the tigers out.

In recent years the emphasis of Project Tiger has changed. More effort is now made to develop the habitat around tiger reserves for local people, in a nondestructive way. This is called ecodevelopment. For example, Project Tiger and other conservation groups work with local people to set up dams and **irrigation** systems so they can get the water they need without taking it from reserves. The groups help install solar-powered lighting around the villages to keep tigers away from people's **livestock.**

Project Tiger

There are now 23 Project Tiger reserves. They make up about one third of the protected areas in which tigers live in India. From 1976–1979, twelve villages were moved when Ranthambhore National Park was set up.

People plant fast-growing plants for fuel and animal feed so they do not have to cut down slow-growing plants in the tiger reserves. These workers are irrigating the fields.

Conservation Organizations

Project Tiger **reserves,** and the national parks in places where Bengal tigers live, need money and expert assistance to keep going. They rely on help from national and local governments and also from international aid. For example, in 1994 the United States Congress passed a Tiger Conservation Act. It gives money to support **development** in other countries that help with tiger conservation.

Tiger conservation also relies on a wide range of nongovernmental organizations (NGOs), including charities. These NGOs may be local, national, or international. Most of these organizations raise money for conservation from donations by the public or businesses. For example, the oil company Exxon pledged over $950,000 to the U.S. Save the Tiger Fund. An NGO called the National Fish and Wildlife Foundation is managing the fund. NGOs and charities sometimes work together with governments. Sometimes they can offer scientific expertise about tigers.

Charities do not make any financial profit from their work. They rely on help from many unpaid volunteers as well as their paid workers. Because they are financially independent, they can protest against government actions that cause **habitat** destruction.

Scientific experts from NGOs and charities study tigers, to help in their conservation. This tiger has been tranquillized so a radio collar can be placed on it.

These traditional medicines advertise that they contain tiger parts. The efforts of conservation organizations have helped to ban their sale.

Conserving Bengal tigers

The tigers' problems have led to the creation of many conservation groups and major **campaigns.** Some have local goals, such as conserving tigers in a particular area, but others are more wide-ranging.

In 1975 the Convention on International Trade in Endangered Species (CITES, pronounced sightease) was formed to control and regulate the trade in **endangered** animals. Campaigns at this time tried to stop people from wearing big-cat fur as fashion, such as fur coats.

More recently, WWF and TRAFFIC worked with the U.S. Congress to establish the 1998 U.S. Rhino and Tiger Product Labeling Act. Just under half of the shops examined in Chinatowns in seven cities in the United States and Canada sold medicines labeled as containing tiger parts. Old laws had made only the distribution of these medicines illegal. The new act made it illegal to sell *any* product containing or claiming to contain tiger parts. In this way, consumers can legally buy only traditional medicines made by responsible manufacturers who do not use illegal ingredients.

How endangered?

Conservation specialists at CITES divide endangered animals into three different categories, depending on how much protection they need. Tigers are ranked CITES Appendix 1, which means they are at risk of **extinction** within five years and any trade in tigers is illegal.

People have caged and enclosed big cats for thousands of years. In the past, zoos simply provided the spectacle of seeing exotic and dangerous animals in cramped cages. The zoos and wildlife parks of today are very different.

Information and conservation

Modern zoos and wildlife parks enable visitors to study tigers close-up, in cages and enclosures that imitate their **habitat.** Visitors can learn more about tigers from information displays, multimedia presentations, and libraries. Money raised from entrance tickets, gift shops, and fundraising is used to look after the captive animals and to help with the conservation of tigers in the wild. Zoos work closely with conservation groups, **reserve** workers, and governments to help look after wild Bengal tigers and their habitats.

Breeding programs

Many zoos have **breeding** programs for **endangered** animals such as tigers. A male from one zoo will be lent to another zoo to mate with a female. Breeding programs are important for providing zoos with enough tigers so that no more are taken from the wild. They also bring money into the zoo from visitors wanting to see baby tigers. This can lead to a surplus of tigers in captivity as zoos breed animals to get this visitor money.

Zoo facts

There are about 1,200 tigers in zoos around the world.

Adult tigers in zoos eat horse meat supplemented with egg, yeast, and vitamins.

Tigers are expensive to keep in captivity. It costs up to $3,100 a year for each tiger.

Captive tigers need keepers to feed them. This cub is being bottle-fed because his mother could not make enough milk.

White tigers are unusual Bengal tigers with creamy white fur, chocolate-brown stripes, and blue eyes.

Tiger breeding programs need to be carefully monitored to avoid **inbreeding.** When any captive tiger breeds with another it is recorded in an internationally-available tiger studbook. Any zoo can then check a tiger's background. There are only around 330 Bengal tigers in captivity, mostly in Indian zoos. Some other tigers identified as Bengals are actually a mixture of Bengal and another tiger **subspecies.**

Reintroduction

Breeding programs are also important for reintroducing some endangered species back into the wild. This is successful for some animals, but not for others. Tigers, like other big cats, cannot be reintroduced. This is mainly because they are **predators.** They survive by hunting. If they have been reared in captivity where they are fed and confined, they will not have learned how to hunt. A reintroduced tiger would also not be resistant to diseases or aware of **territory** and the dangers of other tigers.

white tigers

White tigers are Bengal tigers that are not orange and black! There are around 130 in captivity. Most are inbred **descendants** of a wild white tiger called Mohan, caught in 1951. If a white tiger was born in the wild, it would probably not survive long because its color would not conceal it well when **stalking prey.**

Tiger Tourism and Local People

To see a tiger in the wild would be high on the wish list of many animal lovers. Tiger tourism is an important business in India. Private tour companies, national parks, and **reserves** earn valuable income from tourism. Some of this money helps conserve tigers and other wildlife, but many conservationists say tourism is the latest danger for Bengal tigers.

Tourism can help in the conservation of tigers, but it must be carried out responsibly.

Tourist pressure

Irresponsible tourism can create big problems for tigers, their **habitats,** and the people who live nearby. Visitors demand facilities such as hotels, lodges, and restaurants. These use up local resources such as building materials, water, food, and power, affecting life for local people. The price of these resources and of land sometimes rises so much that local people cannot afford to live there.

Big hotel groups can easily afford to buy land. They often bring their own staff, so they offer no jobs to local people. They contribute little to the local economy. They bring in expensive equipment for the hotels, food for their restaurants, and even forest guides from elsewhere.

Tourism also generates large amounts of waste, such as litter and sewage, that can **pollute** tiger habitat. Increased traffic on roads from private cars and tour buses pollutes the air and increases roadkills. Increased noise from visitors may scare off the wildlife.

Tourists in Periyar benefit from the experience of local guides.

Solutions

Bad tourism operations exclude local people and leave them with problems to clear up. This can make them less caring of tiger habitat and wildlife. These days, a different sort of tourism, called **ecotourism**, is promoted by conservation groups. This is small-scale tourism that involves local people and has a low impact on the environment. If local people get rewards from tourism, they will become the protectors instead of the enemies of nature. Governments sometimes encourage ecotourism by reducing taxes for small-scale tourism and increasing taxes for big hotel groups.

Making tourism work in Periyar

The Periyar National Park in the state of Kerala, India, is home to a pioneering ecotourism project. Local people involved in the Periyar Tiger Trail project used to live in the forest, where they made a living by illegally cutting and selling wild cinnamon bark. They are now partners in the protection of Periyar. They use their detailed knowledge of the area to guide small groups around the reserve. Because they know the area, they are more likely to give visitors the chance to see tigers and other wildlife. The Tiger Trail workers make such a good living from their work that they have become role models for the local community. It is partly because Periyar and its wildlife are valuable to them that there has been no tiger **poaching** in the park since 2000.

The Future for Bengal Tigers

The Bengal tiger is an incredible animal. It has a unique place in the rich and complex natural world in Asia. That world is being changed by people on a larger scale than ever before.

Unfortunately, money is the main problem. Tiger **habitat** is shrinking because lumber and cleared land are worth more money than forests. Tigers are being killed because their bodies can be sold at high prices. At the center of the conservation of tigers is one question: How do you make a live tiger worth more than a dead one, or a habitat with tigers in it worth more than one without them?

Of course, tigers should not need to have a value to be saved. Conservationists argue that people have no right to make any animal **extinct.** However, **ecotourism** is one example of how people can make money from the presence of tigers. It brings in regular income from tourists, year after year. The tourists, therefore, are also helping to conserve tigers.

Trees, tigers, and people

"You can only save tigers by saving forests. And if you save the forests, you also wind up saving the best, purest rivers and lakes ... And when you save your water sources, you save yourself!" Bittu Sahgal, India Wildlife Protection, on the importance of tiger habitat to people.

However many tiger skins and bones are seized, it is poachers' attitudes that need to change for tigers to be really protected.

Tigers are a symbol of wildlife, but also a marker of where we stand as a human civilization. If we cannot save this magnificent creature, what chance is there for helping members of our own **species**, let alone the other species that tigers live among?

Once tigers disappear from a stretch of forest, the will of governments and conservation groups to save that forest from being cut down also often disappears. Then, whole **ecosystems** of animals and plants that have developed over millions of years disappear.

The Tiger State

In 1994 Madhya Pradesh was named The Tiger State because of the number of tigers there, the number of **reserves,** and the area of suitable tiger habitat. The state set up a Tiger Cell, combining the efforts of police and forest officers to seize **poached** items. Since then, this possible model of tiger conservation has failed because of corruption. Officials have allowed large areas of forest habitat to be destroyed. For example, there are around 10,000 sawmills, half of which are illegal, that process newly cut forest trees. Although a tiger count in 1997 showed a rise in tiger numbers since the previous count, closer investigation showed that numbers had in fact dropped and that the original count was deliberately false.

The problems Bengal tigers face are so great that it seems impossible that any individual can help them. However, if you want to help save tigers, you can make a difference.

Learn more

You can read books, watch TV programs, and visit sites on the Internet. A good starting point might be your local library. How about learning about tigers as part of a class project?

Write a letter

People in government in India and other countries where Bengal tigers live make many decisions that affect tigers. For example, they make laws that control land use and employ the police and **reserve wardens** who try to stop **poaching.** Governments in countries around the world can influence the use of and trade in traditional medicines containing tiger parts. Governments are more likely to make the right decisions for tigers if they receive letters from people concerned about them.

There are various letter-writing **campaigns** you can contribute to. For example, the Save The Tiger Fund encourages letters to the prime minister of India. On its website, the organization provides information to include in your letter and the address to send it to. You can also write your own letter and get others who agree with you to sign it. This is called a petition. People who sign it should also clearly write their name and indicate where they are from.

The more you know about Bengal tigers, the more you can tell others about their problems. These school children are learning about tigers and other animals in Corbett National Park, India.

> *Just doing something, however small it may be, is a thousand times better than doing nothing.*

Jenny's petition

Jenny Osgood of Cornwall, United Kingdom, learned that there were at most 7,000 tigers of all **subspecies** left on Earth. She felt very angry about this, and in particular about poaching to provide materials for traditional medicines. So, she started a petition. She left copies of the petition in local shops and gas stations. She also went with her family into her local town and asked people she met on the street to sign the petition. Within ten weeks Jenny had collected 7,000 signatures, one for every **endangered** tiger. She sent the petition to the UK Environmental Investigation Agency. They were so impressed that they asked Jenny to take the petition herself to the Indian prime minister, Mr. I.K. Gujral. Mr. Gujral said his government was committed to saving the tiger.

Jenny's petition started a children's campaign in India and worldwide. It was coordinated by conservation groups including Tiger Link and WWF-India. There are already a 250,000 signatures, and organizers are aiming for one million.

Donations

Many people help Bengal tigers by giving money. Some schools and individuals have "adopted" a tiger. This means they pay money to help conserve a particular tiger and receive information about it. You do not have to give much money. For example, you can donate subscriptions to *Cub* magazine to schoolchildren in India for around 60 cents a year. Their families usually cannot afford to buy them their own subscription. *Cub* is a great way for kids who live near tigers to learn more about them and get involved locally in their conservation.

ancestor   one from whom an individual has descended. For example, your grandparents and great-grandparents are your ancestors.

breed   produce babies

campaign   organized activity to bring about change

carcass   dead body of an animal

carnivore   animal that eats other animals

colonizers   people from one place who take over another place

customs   officials who control the movement of goods between different countries

deciduous   trees that lose all their leaves at particular times of the year

descendant   offspring. For example, you are a descendant of your grandparents.

development   change that is supposed to improve land or habitat

ecosystem   all the living and nonliving things in a particular area

ecotourism   a kind of tourism that aims to benefit habitats, wildlife, and local people

endangered   when a plant or animal is in danger of dying out

extinct   no longer living on Earth

food web   diagram that shows the paths by which food energy is passed from plants to animals

genes   parts of living cells that control how an organism looks and how it will survive, grow, and change through its life

genus   a classification grouping. In the genus *Panthera*, the big cats, there are several species. In the cat family there are several genera.

glands   small, specialized structures in various parts of the body

habitat   place in the natural world where a particular organism lives

herbivore   animal that eats plants

home range   area within a habitat in which an animal usually lives

inbreeding   when animals that are closely related make babies

irrigation   supply water to the land and crops

livestock   animals kept for meat or milk, or to be sold

mammal   warm-blooded animal with hair and a backbone that can feed its young with milk from its body

mark   sign left by an animal. For example, one animal leaves a scent mark to show other animals where its territory is.

monsoon   tropical rainy season in Asia

poach   catch or kill an animal illegally

pollution   poisoning or harming of the environment by human activity

predator   animal that hunts, kills, and eats other animals

prey   animal that is hunted and eaten by another animal

reserve   area of protected land where animals and plants live safely

retina   thin layer at the back of the eye that reacts to light

scrub   dry habitat that often has thorny, low-growing plants

smuggle   transport something illegally, usually across borders of countries

species   group of living things that are similar and can reproduce together to produce healthy offspring

stalk   closely follow prey in order to get close enough to catch it

subspecies   distinct type that can breed with other subspecies within a species. For example, Bengal tigers are a subspecies of tiger.

suckle   when a baby mammal drinks milk from its mother's body

suffocate   prevent from breathing

territory   particular area an animal claims and defends as its own

track   follow marks such as pugmarks (footprints) to locate an animal

tropical   area close to the equator where it is very hot

warden   person paid to guard a particular area, such as a reserve

water catchment area   area into which a lot of rainwater falls and collects in rivers and lakes

Conservation groups and websites

All these groups work to help conserve all five **subspecies** of tigers, including Bengal tigers. You can find out much more, including addresses and details about particular projects or fundraising, by visiting their websites.

WWF

www.panda.org

WWF (the World Wildlife Fund) is a large global organization committed to protecting the natural world. Tigers are one of their flagship **species.** These are recognizable animals that inspire conservation not only of tigers but also of their **habitats.** WWF has just launched a new conservation strategy and action plan to conserve different tiger habitats.

Save The Tiger Fund

www.5tigers.org

This giant U.S. charity has spent more than $10 million on tiger conservation since 1995. It sponsors The Tiger Information Center's 5 Tigers website, which is one of the major places to find tiger information. It also provides links to other conservation organizations. You can use this site to find out details about writing protest letters.

IUCN – The World Conservation Union

lynx.uio.no/catfolk

The Cat Specialist Group is a team of scientists and wildlife managers from around the world with experience and knowledge of tigers. They are one group within IUCN. Their website has lots of details about all types of cats, including tigers.

TRAFFIC

www.traffic.org

TRAFFIC is an international trade control program set up by WWF and IUCN. Their website details several initiatives to stop tiger **smuggling.**

Project Tiger

envfor.nic.in/pt/tcroom/tcroom.html

This Indian government site contains links to the Project Tiger reserves across India and detailed information about the status of tigers in these reserves.

Other Indian conservation groups

There are many other dedicated tiger conservation groups in India. Here are just a few:

Tiger Trust
www.indiantiger.com/trust/index

Wildlife Protection Society of India
www.wpsi-india.org

The Wildlife Trust of India
www.wildlifetrustofindia.org

The Corbett Foundation
www.corbettfoundation.org

Books

Chaterjee, Manini and Anita Roy. *Eyewitness: India.* New York: DK
    Publishing, 2002.

Gentle, Victor and Janet Perry. *Tigers.* Milwaukee, Wis.: Gareth Stevens,
    2002.

Vogel, Elizabeth. *Tigers.* New York: Powerkids Press, 2002.

Wexo, John. *Big Cats.* San Diego, Calif.: Zoobooks/Wildlife Education,
    2001.

Index